THE METS FAN'S
LITTLE BOOK OF WISDOM

Other "Little Books of Wisdom" Titles Available

THE METS FAN'S
LITTLE BOOK OF WISDOM

Bucky Fox

Taylor Trade Publishing
Lanham • New York • Boulder • Toronto • Oxford

Published by Taylor Trade Publishing
An imprint of The Rowman & Littlefield Publishing Group, Inc.
4501 Forbes Boulevard, Suite 200, Lanham, Maryland 20706

Distributed by NATIONAL BOOK NETWORK

Library of Congress Cataloging-in-Publication Data

Fox, Bucky.
  The Mets fan's little book of wisdom / Bucky Fox.— 1st Taylor Trade Pub. ed.
    p. cm.
  ISBN 1-58979-301-3 (pbk. : alk. paper)
  1. New York Mets (Baseball team)—Anecdotes. 2. New York Mets (Baseball team)—Humor. I. Title.
  GV875.N45F59 2006
  796.357'64097471—dc22   2005027896

∞™ The paper used in this publication meets the minimum requirements of American National Standard for Information Sciences—Permanence of Paper for Printed Library Materials, ANSI/NISO Z39.48-1992. Manufactured in the United States of America.

Dedication

To Charles Dickens Fox, an All-Star at all the positions—father, friend, Army war hero—and a major sports fan who dumped the Dodgers when they fled New York and taught me to root for the new home team, the Mets.

And to Bob Wicker, an amazing sports editor at the soldier newspaper *Stars & Stripes* who put up with me even after his beloved Red Sox fell to my Mets in 1986.

Introduction

How do you translate New York Mets fan?

It means:

- Laughing at Jimmy Piersall for running backward around the bases after hitting his 100th career home run in the Mets' early joke era.
- Cheering Ron Swoboda for doubling in the championship run of the Mets' miracle 1969 season.
- Grieving Gil Hodges' death in 1972.
- Welcoming back Willie Mays to New York in 1972.
- Believing in the Mets' pennant sprint of 1973.
- Disbelieving the Mets' trade of Tom Seaver in 1977.
- Optimism after the Mets' pickup of Keith Hernandez in 1983.
- Grasping the potential of the Mets' Double D, Darryl Strawberry, and Doc Gooden in 1984.

- Seeing a pending title upon the Mets' trade for Gary Carter before the 1985 season.
- Happy days during Ray Knight's World Series MVP performance for the Mets in 1986.
- Losing it while watching Jay Payton's winning hits for the Mets in the 2000 playoffs.
- Reliving so much Mets history through the Web sites UltimateMets.com, Baseball-Reference.com, BaseballLibrary.com, and TheBaseballPage.com while researching this book.
- Trying to make this Mets book as clean as a David Wright double in 2005, thanks to the eagle eyes of my sister Debbie King and my buddy Tony Batt.
- Hoping the Mets win another World Series.

Bucky Fox
October 2005

Let's Get Our Priorities Straight

"The last miracle I did was the 1969 Mets. Before that, I think you have to go back to the Red Sea." Who said it? God in the 1977 movie *Oh, God!*

Before the Dessert Comes, Talk about Something Important

How obsessed can New York Mets fans be? Plenty, as captured in an early 1970s New Yorker cartoon.

The scene: a restaurant.

The characters: man and woman.

Man: "Enough about me. Let's talk about the Mets."

Follow Yogi's Lead

Yogi Berra managed the 1973 Mets to one of the great comebacks in history. On July 31, they stood dead last in the NL East. Berra hardly flinched. He responded with his most memorable observation: "It ain't over till it's over."

Indeed it wasn't. The Mets came alive, going 38-22 and overcoming a 10½-game deficit to capture the division title.

Sometimes When You're Near, You're Really Far

Through the 2005 season, no Mets pitcher had tossed a no-hitter. Boy, did they come close on July 9, 1969. Tom Seaver mowed down the Cubs one after another. With one out in the ninth, he had a perfect game. Up stepped Jimmy Qualls, who ruined the gem with a single to left-center. That didn't stop Seaver from calling his book *The Perfect Game*.

Break Up Laughing
(If It Hurts Too Much)

In 1965, the Mets were the laughing stock of baseball. They were on their way to their fourth straight last-place finish.

Midseason they held Banner Day. Fans traipsed out banners between games of a doubleheader with the Cubs. The best one: "Break Up the Mets." The Mets stayed together long enough to go 50-112.

Sometimes You Want to Pray for Thanks

Cleon Jones was the first great offensive Met. His .340 average helped power the 1969 Amazin's to the top. And his defensive play clinched it. It came on Davey Johnson's fly to left with two out in Game 5 of the World Series. Jones camped under it, caught it, kneeled and acknowledged the miracle world title.

Heads Up

Casey Stengel, after rookie Ron Swoboda tore up the dugout in 1965: "If everybody on this team commenced breaking up the furniture every time we did bad, there'd be no place to sit."

Keeping Hitting, Even After the Game

Joel Youngblood had one busy baseball day on August 4, 1982. In the afternoon, he singled for the Mets in Chicago. That didn't do him much good. The Mets told him in the middle of the game that they had traded him to the Montreal Expos. So Youngblood packed up and joined his new team that night in Philadelphia, where he promptly produced a hit. He thus became the first player to collect hits for two teams in two cities on the same day.

Coming Back Can Give You Multiple Jitters

The Mets won the National League East in 1986 in a rout. They had to bounce off the mat to win the world championship. Everyone remembers their incredible comeback in Game 6 of the World Series. But many forget their desperate rally in Game 6 of the National League playoffs. They scored three in the 9th to tie it and three more in the 16th before holding off the Houston Astros 7-6.

Smile, the Ryan Express
Was Once in Our Station

Nolan Ryan notched his Hall of Fame and legendary strikeout credentials with the Angels, Astros and Rangers. Then again, he never won a title with any of them. He did with the Mets. He pitched seven innings of relief in Game 3 of the 1969 playoffs to clinch the pennant, then helped beat Baltimore in the World Series. By 1972, the Mets had traded him in maybe their worst blunder.

A Dynasty Can Die in Nasty Fashion

The 1988 Mets were close to making it two world titles in three years. Taking a cue from the '86 champs, the '88 bunch compiled the best record in the National League. They were about to take a 3-1 series lead against the Dodgers in the NL playoffs. The Mets led 4-2 with one out in the ninth, and that moment proved to be the peak of Met power. The lights went out fast. Doc Gooden delivered to Mike Scioscia, who homered to tie it, and Los Angeles won in the 12th. The Dodgers finished off the Mets in seven games and went on to win the World Series. The Mets meandered through the dark for over a decade before reaching the World Series again.

Homers Make for a Fine Wake-Up Call

The Mets sleepwalked through the early part of the 2005 season. They staggered to 0-5. A couple of weeks later, the alarm sounded. They jumped up and hammered seven home runs at Philadelphia in a 16-4 bell-ringing of the Phillies. Hitting the club-record, magnificent seven were Jose Reyes and Victor Diaz with two each, David Wright, Mike Piazza and Doug Mientkiewicz.

Keep Your Focused Eyes on the Ball

Jason Phillips opened the 2003 season as the Mets catcher, what with Mike Piazza suspended. Phillips shifted to first base, what with Mo Vaughn finished. Phillips lasted two seasons in New York and will forever be remembered for his goggles. Shades of Clint Courtney, the 1950s catcher for the St. Louis Browns who pioneered the rare look of glasses behind the plate.

Father's Day Can Be Perfect

Take Father's Day in 1964. Please. It sure was perfect for fatherly fans of the Philadelphia Phillies. Their Jim Bunning pitched a perfect game that day against the Mets at Shea Stadium. A few weeks after that 27-up, 27-down fog, the franchise showed off its sunny, new digs in the All-Star Game.

Cross-Town Doesn't Mean Uptown

Joe Torre will reach the Hall of Fame because of his stellar managerial career in New York. That is, with the Yankees, with whom he's won four World Series titles. Not with the Mets, with whom he bombed. Torre switched from player to manager in the middle of the 1977 season. He produced a miserable .405 record until losing the job after the 1981 season.

16

There's Always an Award

Roberto Alomar didn't pan out as a Met. After hitting .336, with 20 homers and 100 runs batted in for the 2001 Cleveland Indians, he landed in New York with hopes of solidifying second base and the plate. He flopped, hitting .266 with 11 homers and 53 RBI to help the 2002 Mets fall to the cellar. Still, in September at Shea, Alomar heard huzzahs. That's because the Puerto Rican received the Latino MVP award for the previous season.

17

Sometimes Mope Can Lead to Hope

The Mets traded Tom Seaver to the Cincinnati Reds in a deal that left New Yorkers crushed. Mets fans loved Tom Terrific from his Rookie of the Year days of 1967 to his Cy Young performances of 1969, '73 and '75. But by '77 he wanted more money and wanted to split. After he beat Houston 3-1 on June 12, he hung his head in the Astrodome clubhouse while sportswriters whispered around him. The Mets got the message and shipped him to the Reds three days later. He went 14-3 the rest of the way with Cincy and stuck it to New York fans by beating the Mets in his return to Shea.

You Can Go Home Again

Six years after he left New York, Tom Seaver returned to the team that made him a superstar. He donned Mets pinstripes and showed his old greatness on opening day at Shea, tossing six innings of shutout ball on April 5, 1983. Doug Sisk cleaned up and collected the win in the Mets' 2-0 triumph.

But the Stay at Home Can Be Short

Tom Seaver's second stint with the Mets lasted just one season. After he went 9-14 in 1983, they left him unprotected in a replacement draft, and the Chicago White Sox grabbed him.

Seaver was hardly through. Over the next two years he went 31-22, which included win No. 300. At least that landmark game came in New York—against the Yankees.

By 1986 he was with the other Sox. And although he wasn't activated for the World Series, he was in Boston's dugout watching the Mets win it all.

Remember the Voice of Summer

Bob Murphy broadcast Mets games from their birth to 2003. He died the next year. One of his greatest calls came on October 25, 1986, the night the Mets leapt off the mat to beat Boston in Game 6 of the World Series: "Mookie Wilson still hopes to win it for New York . . . 3-2 the count . . . and the pitch by Stanley . . . and a ground ball trickling. . . . It's a fair ball. It gets by Buckner! Rounding third is Knight. . . . The Mets will win the ballgame. . . . They win! They win!"

Sometimes Rain Is a Losing Element

Early in the 2005 season, the Mets protested a rain-shortened loss in Washington. The visitors claimed that the grounds crew at RFK Stadium took too long to cover the field. Mets manager Willie Randolph took this shot: "I thought that they were understaffed and undermanned." Larry Stewart of the *Los Angeles Times* penned this zinger: "What did the Mets expect? Rarely does anything get done in a timely fashion in Washington."

Discover the Art of the Deal

A generation after the Mets' infamous trades of Nolan Ryan and Tom Seaver, they found a way to trade for a franchise stud. On May 22, 1998, they turned truly Amazin' by hooking Mike Piazza from the Florida Marlins. All they gave up for maybe the greatest hitting catcher of all time were Preston Wilson, Ed Yarnall and Geoff Goetz. Two years later, the Mets were in the World Series, thanks to that deal.

Sound Off After the Fans Tune In

Lindsey Nelson—he of the loud jacket—was in the Mets broadcast booth from the start. He lasted until 1978 and died 17 years later. He called one of the greatest moments in Mets history. It came on September 24, 1969, when they clinched the National League East title: "This could be it. There's one, there's two, the Mets are the champions. At 9:07 on September 24th, the New York Mets clinched the Eastern Division of the National League. Look at that scene. Gentry's cap is gone. It's a scene of wild jubilation."

24

A Broken Bat Can Equal Broken Spirits

The Mets entered Game 2 of the 2000 Subway Series planning to splinter the Yankees' dynasty. So in the first inning, the Mets' No. 1 slugger, Mike Piazza, swung mightily against the Yanks' No. 1 pitcher, Roger Clemens. Piazza connected, but the bat shattered and flew right at Clemens. The pitcher picked up the jagged barrel and threw it at Piazza. Did the Mets catcher react like a leader and barrel into Clemens? No. Piazza did nothing. Later he said, "It's all irrelevant." Except that the Mets broke down after that and lost the Series four games to one.

Later Can Come Fast

Harry Chiti landed on the Mets in April 1962 in a trade with the Cleveland Indians for a player to be named later. Who did that player turn out to be? Chiti. The Mets shipped him back to the Indians a few weeks later as the player to be named later. What does that mean? Chiti was traded for himself.

Keep Swinging Through the Air

Ralph Kiner joined Lindsey Nelson and Bob Murphy in the Mets broadcast booth in 1962. Kiner quickly connected with his voice the way he did with his bat as a Hall of Fame slugger. He also voiced a few disconnects, such as:

"If Casey Stengel were alive today, he'd be spinning in his grave."

"The Mets have gotten their leadoff batter on only once this inning."

"Now up to bat for the Mets is Gary Cooper."

When You're Out, Out, Out, Out

Kelvin Chapman played second base for the Mets in the lean season of 1979 and rejoined the team for the uptrend campaigns of 1984 and '85. His batting numbers are nondescript. But he did pull off a cycle. He didn't hit for one. He ran for one—getting thrown out at every base in one game.

It Takes Bats to Beat Back Power

The 1969 Mets sped to a 100-62 record, best in the National League. That would've been their ticket to the World Series before that season, but this was the dawn of divisions and playoffs. So they faced the Atlanta Braves in the first National League Championship Series. The Braves boasted Hank Aaron, and he delivered three homers against the pitching-rich Mets. New York's answer? Runs. The Mets routed Atlanta in the three-game set 9-5, 11-6 and 7-4.

It Helps To Be Hot
When It Counts

Wayne Garrett joined the Mets in 1969 and hit one homer in the regular season. He left the team in the middle of the '76 season after lofting four dingers. In between, he never hit higher than .256. But man, did this third baseman heat up at pressure points. Take his rookie year. In Game 3 of the NL playoffs, his two-run homer clinched the pennant. In 1973 he pounded the ball down the stretch as the Mets overcame St. Louis and Pittsburgh for the division title. And in the World Series, his homer in Game 3 gave the Mets a lead that, if Tom Seaver had held it, could have vaulted them to the championship.

Stir the Drink
and Enjoy the Party

Darryl Strawberry was the prime swashbuckler in a Mets gang that swaggered through the mid-'80s. He flexed his power on the field and his party side off it. Borrowing from Reggie Jackson, Straw stirred the drink. Mets fans will forever remember Strawberry's sweetest blow of the regular season. It came on October 1, 1985. The Mets were in St. Louis and desperately trying to catch the Cardinals in the NL East. On came the 11th inning. Two out. Up stepped Strawberry. The pitch. Goodbye. Straw's shot rocketed to the clock behind the bleachers in right-center. The Mets held on for a 1-0 triumph.

This Is a Time to Show Off

The Mets couldn't quite catch St. Louis in the 1985 race. In '86, they lapped the Cards. And won everything. Darryl Strawberry came through like a true front-runner. His Scud missile shot in the eighth inning of Game 7 locked up the Mets' second World Series title. Amid the launch, Straw stirred slowly around the bases—to make sure Boston knew who stood tall.

Sometimes a Player Is That Great

He had the juicy name: Strawberry. He had the sweet start: 26 homers in his 1983 Rookie of the Year season. He had the lush decade, helping the Mets to the 1986 world championship and '88 NL East title. How good was he? Broadcaster Ralph Kiner put it this way: "Darryl Strawberry has been voted to the Hall of Fame five years in a row."

Take the Gooden with the Badder

Dwight Gooden was as good as it gets. For three seasons. In his blazing Rookie of the Year campaign of 1984, he cut down 276 batters in just 218 innings, claiming the Doctor K moniker. In 1985, he gripped the Cy Young Award with a mega 24-4, 1.53 ERA, 268-strikeout performance. In 1986, even with lighter numbers, he pitched the Mets to the world title. He was a lock for the Hall of Fame. Only injuries and drugs unlocked that shot and slammed the door on his career.

One Is the Loneliest (and Most Frustrating) Number

Like Tom Seaver, Doc Gooden came this close to tossing the Mets' first no-hitter. It came during his rocket rookie rise in 1984. On September 7, with the Mets homing in on the Cubs for the NL East lead, Gooden fired a one-hitter at Shea. It would have been a gem except that third baseman Ray Knight bobbled a slow roller in the fifth inning and couldn't throw out the slower Keith Moreland. An error would have preserved Gooden's no-no, but the scorer ruled it a hit. The Mets did win 10-0, but failed to catch Chicago down the stretch.

Carry a Big Stick and Break It

Carlos Baerga came over to the Mets from Cleveland late in the 1996 season with a smashing image. In 424 at bats with the Indians, he broke his stick 96 times. That's twice the major league average. The infielder didn't get much wood on the ball with his new team. He hit just .193 in 26 games with the Mets the rest of '96.

It's All in the Look

The Mets often wear black and blue these days. When they started out in 1962, their garb stuck with orange and blue. Why all those combinations? Those were the colors of their New York National League predecessors, the Giants and Dodgers.

Laugh It Up

The comical Mets played in one of the funniest movies, 1968's *The Odd Couple*. They face Pittsburgh at Shea, with Walter Matthau's Oscar Madison in the press box between sportswriters Heywood Hale Broun and Maury Allen. The Pirates' Bill Mazeroski steps up.

Broun: "Bases loaded. Mazeroski up. Ninth inning. You expect the Mets to hold a one-run lead?"

Oscar: "Whatsa matter? You never heard of a triple play?"

He proceeds to turn his back to take a call from Jack Lemmon's Felix Ungar, who gives crucial advice about dinner.

Broun: "A triple play! The Mets did it! The greatest fielding play I ever saw! And you missed it, Oscar. You missed it!"

Don't Worry, It's a Long Season

The Mets opened their eighth season on April 8, 1969, in familiar fashion. The perennial losers lost 11-10 at Shea. Only this was particularly embarrassing. The team that beat them was the Montreal Expos in their very first game. What, the Mets worry? They merely dusted themselves off and cleaned up on all of baseball the next six months.

The Great Ones Catch On

Gary Carter shares plenty with Yogi Berra. Both caught for the Mets. Both wore No. 8. Both reached the Hall of Fame. And both share this record: homering in four straight opening day games. They pulled their opening day power feat before joining the Mets: Carter with the Expos from 1977 to '80, Berra with the Yankees from 1955 to '58. Then came another catcher to join that opening day grand slam: Todd Hundley, who went yard from 1994 to '97, all as a Met.

Make Your Mark

The Mets contended in 1984, but needed one more piece to complete the championship puzzle. Enter Gary Carter. They traded for the All-Star catcher in the off-season, and he quickly showed why they went after him. On opening day, April 9, 1985, he beat the Cardinals with a home run in the 10th inning at Shea. The fans celebrated their new hero's winner with "Gary! Gary! Gary!" They would finish behind St. Louis in the division that season, but the Mets were getting close.

When Your Back's Against the Wall, Homer Over It

Gary Carter wasn't just an opening day star. He also came through at the end for the Mets. Take Game 4 of the 1986 World Series. With the Mets down two games to one, Carter skied two homers over the Green Monster at Boston's Fenway Park in a 6-2 New York triumph.

Never Give Up

The Mets could've said forget it in Game 6 of the 1986 World Series. They trailed 5-3 with two out in the 10th inning at Shea. One more out, and the Boston Red Sox would have been champions. But the Mets remembered who the best team was. "I just knew when I came to the plate that I was going to get on base somehow," Gary Carter told the *CoopersTown Crier* years later. "I just felt like that was our year, and I never felt like we were going to lose." So Carter singled, the Mets scored three times to win, then clinched the title in Game 7.

Winning Sounds So Good

Bob Murphy's call on October 27, 1986: "Now the pitch on the way. . . . He struck him out! . . . Struck him out! The Mets have won the World Series! The dream has come true. The Mets have won the World Series, coming from behind to win the seventh game."

Make Sure Your Boss Is Having Fun

Manager Casey Stengel was the John Wooden and Vince Lombardi of baseball. He won seven World Series titles, including a stunning five straight from 1949 to '53. They all came with the Yankees. Stengel's tenure with the Mets had a different tone: short on wins and long on jokes. His teams from 1962 to '65 played dreadfully. So he resorted to one-liners. Such as: "The only thing worse than a Mets game is a Mets doubleheader." And while referring to President Johnson, "He wanted to see poverty, so he came to see my team."

Build It, and Fans Will Come

They were more Mess than Mets early on. From 1962 to '65, their average record was 49-113. Yet New York fans were so hungry for National League baseball, they consumed their new team. Mets attendance passed 1 million in 1963, and that was at the old Polo Grounds. When Shea Stadium opened the next year, fans flocked to the tune of 1.7 million, way over the league average and more than the American League champion Yankees. In 1965, despite the Mets' 50-112 disaster, attendance reached 1.8 million.

Try to Manage the Destruction

The Mets stumbled through their first two seasons of 1962 and 1963 with a .283 winning percentage, although there was nothing winning about it. They pulled off that stunt at the Polo Grounds in Manhattan before moving to Queens.

"At the end of this season they're gonna tear this place down," Casey Stengel told one of his pitchers in that last Polo campaign. "The way you're pitchin', that right-field section will be gone already."

Say Shea,
and You Know You're Home

Shea Stadium has a familiar ring after all these years. So who was Shea, anyway? He was William Shea, an attorney instrumental in filling the National League void in New York after the Dodgers and Giants left after the 1957 season.

Shea Loves You

Construction on the stadium started in 1961, and it was going to be called Flushing Meadows Park. That changed to Shea Stadium by the time it opened on April 17, 1964. Even more than the World Series clinching games of 1969 and '86, Shea's loudest moment came on August 15, 1965. That night the Beatles rocked the stadium filled with nearly 60,000 screamers.

Dream of Being a Giant

The Mets did more than give New York a National League team after a four-year stretch from 1958 to '61 when the city had only the Yankees. The Amazin's also helped fans remember their old favorites with their colors. Did they lean more toward the Giants or Dodgers? Maybe the former, since the Mets took the same logo as the one on the caps of John McGraw, Carl Hubbell, and Willie Mays.

Have a Hall of a Good Time

The Mets won the world championship twice: 1969 and 1986. Three players from those teams have plaques in the Hall of Fame up the road in Cooperstown: Tom Seaver and Nolan Ryan from the Miracle Mets, and Gary Carter from the later version.

You Don't Have to Spell It Out

What's with New York's National League name? The team was actually born the Metropolitans, which was taken from the city's team of the 1880s. That old bunch often went by Mets, and so does this one, whose official name is the New York Metropolitan Baseball Club.

Sometimes You Can Triple the Pain

How badly did the Mets end their first season?

This badly: In their last game of 1962, against the Chicago Cubs on September 30 at Wrigley Field, the Mets' Joe Pignatano stepped up with two on and no outs in the eighth inning. He sank to the occasion by hitting into a triple play.

The Mets lost 5-1. They finished 80 games under .500. They placed 18 games behind those ninth-place Cubs. And Pignatano became the first major leaguer to hit into a triple play in his last at bat.

Months before in spring training, Stengel was asked, "Where do you think the Mets will finish?" His reply: "We'll finish in Chicago."

You Can Always Use a Lift

Elio Chacon came from Venezuela and threw his muscles around the Big Apple. Or tried. The little shortstop played on the 1962 Mets and figured he would spark his hapless club by fighting baseball's Giant, Willie Mays. The brawl climaxed with Mays chucking Chacon to the side. The Caracas contender was out of the majors after that season.

Believe While You're Still Looking Up

The Mets went to spring training in St. Petersburg, Florida, in 1969 with nary a thing to believe in. Their finishes since expansion were last, last, last, last, second to last, last and second to last. First? Who possibly believed in that? Their catcher. "In spring training Jerry Grote knew. He said we were going to win it. We thought he was crazy, nuts. But it made sense. He was the one who had caught us all the year before and he was catching us now in spring training. He just knew." So said Tom Seaver, who went on to pitch those Amazin's to the championship.

Leave Your Mark Any Way You Can

The Mets' first manager, Casey Stengel, knew talent when he saw it: "You couldn't play on the Amazin' Mets without having held some kind of record. Like one fella held the world's international all-time record for a catcher getting hit on the ankles."

Do Something Unique

You could say Donn Clendenon made the Mets champions in 1969. But not before this Donn One pulled a stunt as unusual as that double "n." In January he refused to leave Montreal in a trade to the Houston Astros. Commissioner Bowie Kuhn relented, and Clendenon stayed with the Expos.

That is, until midseason. That's when the Expos traded Clendenon to New York. This time he agreed, and he proceeded to ignite the Mets.

At crunch time, and the former Pirate crested with a World Series Most Valuable Player performance: three home runs and a .357 average in the Mets' five-game triumph over Baltimore.

You Can Be Almost the Most Valuable

No Met was voted National League Most Valuable Player heading into the 2006 season. Yet one got as close as you can get.

The year was 1969, and Tom Seaver pitched one terrific season. His 25-7 record, 2.21 earned-run average and 208 strikeouts armed the Mets against all comers. The baseball writers were so impressed, they gave Seaver as many first-place votes as Willie McCovey, the home run and RBI champion of the San Francisco Giants. Seaver lost out for the award because of McCovey's stronger overall balloting.

Seaver's consolation? The Cy Young Award, which he won nearly unanimously. The only other first-place vote went to Atlanta's Phil Niekro.

You Could Add It Up

Casey Stengel: "I got a kid, Greg Goosen, he's 19 years old, and in 10 years he's got a chance to be 29."

Goosen was a catcher on Stengel's last team, 1965, and lasted with the Mets through 1968. Goosen missed the Mets' magical 1969, but he stayed in the entertainment business many years. Shifting toward acting, he had movie parts in *Get Shorty*, *Behind Enemy Lines*, and, naturally, *Mr. Baseball*.

Marvelous Doesn't Always Mean It

The standard-bearer of the Mets' 1962 flop was Marvelous Marv Throneberry. He drew his nickname for the very reason the team was called Amazin'. It dripped with irony.

The Marvelous one bumbled in the field and on the base paths that first Mets season. He fit right in, what with his initials spelling MET.

Sportswriter Jack Lang put it this way after Throneberry was called out for missing first: "How could he be expected to remember where the bases were? He gets on so infrequently."

You Can Have Your Cake If You Can Catch It

Casey Stengel, to fielding marvel Marv Throneberry on his birthday: "We was going to get you a birthday cake, but we figured you'd drop it."

Home Runs Can Get Depressing—For the Loser

One of the great home run hitters in Mets history was Dave Kingman. He especially displayed his power on June 4, 1976, by clobbering three homers in an 11-0 rout of the Los Angeles Dodgers. King Kong's hat trick left Dodger coach Tommy Lasorda's head spinning: "What's my opinion of Kingman's performance!? What the BLEEP do you think is my opinion of it? I think it was BLEEPING BLEEP."

Catch On If You Can

Casey Stengel, on his three Mets catchers: "I got one that can throw but can't catch, and one that can catch but can't throw, and one who can hit but can't do either." And Casey mispronouncing Chris Cannizzaro: "He's a remarkable catcher, that Canzoneri. He's the only defensive catcher in baseball who can't catch."

63

Stop Dropping and Start Lifting

Davey Johnson might have been the Mets' greatest manager. He took over in 1984 after the Mets had suffered through seven straight losing seasons. He won at once. This was a man who had the last hit against Sandy Koufax. And, also as a Baltimore Oriole, made the last out of the 1969 World Series. He knew how to leave his mark. Johnson had the smarts to bring along Dwight Gooden from their Tidewater minor league days. In that rookie year for both, the Mets won 90 games and contended for the NL East title. They won 98 the next year and nearly won the division. Then came 1986. With Johnson calling the shots, the Mets went 108-54, one of the great records of all time. They sweat through historical Game 6s in the playoffs and World Series and won it all.

Valentine Meant Hearty Seasons

Bobby Valentine nearly duplicated the success of Davey Johnson. Like Johnson, Valentine dug the Mets out of a rut. New York trudged through 103 losses in 1993, hired Valentine in '96, and the next two seasons he had them up and running at 88-74. Like Johnson, Valentine twice managed the Mets to the postseason, including one World Series. Bobby's boys pushed Atlanta to six games in the 1999 NL Championship Series. By 2000, the Mets were in the World Series, losing to the Yankees in five games.

65

Bad Can Be the Worst

The 1962 Mets set the modern baseball record for futility. They went 40-120—60 1/2 games out of first place—and it could have been worse. They had one tie and a rainout they didn't bother to make up.

The Mets were so bad, they went 3-13 against the National League's other expansion team, the Houston Colt .45s.

Then again, if you go back-back-back, the 1899 Cleveland Spiders undercut the Mets. The Spiders spun an ugly web of 20-134, 84 games out of first.

Also in the misery loves company department, the 2003 Detroit Tigers nearly revisited 1962 by bumbling to 43-119.

Even When You're Down, Your Place Can Be Up

Shea Stadium was brand new in 1964, but the Mets were their old selves—headed for over 100 losses and last place again. Still, Shea stood above all of baseball one day—July 7 for the All-Star Game. Nearly 51,000 witnessed one of the most thrilling Midsummer Classics of all time. Down 4-3 in the ninth, the National League rallied to tie it when Orlando Cepeda drove in Willie Mays, then won it 7-4 on Johnny Callison's two-out, three-run homer. The lone New York National Leaguer was Ron Hunt, the first Met elected to an All-Star Game. The second baseman went one for three.

67

When You Hear Gil, Think of Will

Gil Hodges' 14 is one of three numbers the Mets retired. The others are Casey Stengel's 37 and Tom Seaver's 41. Stengel was the Mets' first manager, Seaver probably their greatest player.

And Hodges? The man who hit the Mets' first home run gave them real power—the power to believe they could win. After an early stint as the Mets' first baseman, Hodges took over as manager in 1968. He quickly gave them 73-89 respectability. Then came 1969. With Hodges as solid as his old Brooklyn bat, the Mets rallied from 9 1/2 games back in August to win the NL East by eight games toward the world championship.

Hodges might have stayed the Mets' skipper another decade. But on Easter Sunday 1972, he died of a heart attack after playing golf. He was two days shy of his 48th birthday.

Sing Your Team a Greeting

The Mets were so lovable in their early losing years, they played to a song. Bill Katz and Ruth Roberts wrote it in 1963, and *Meet the Mets* lives as baseball's most famous song after *Take Me out to the Ballgame.* Part of it:

Oh, the butcher and the baker and the people on the streets, where did they go? To MEET THE METS!

Oh, they're hollerin' and cheerin' and they're jumpin' in their seats, where did they go? To MEET THE METS!

Stay Out Late and Have a Grand Time

The Mets won one of the longest postseason game in history. It was Game 5 of the 1999 NL Championship Series, and nearly six hours of baseball left the fans at Shea hysterical because the home team pulled out an Amazin' finish. Down 3-2 to Atlanta in the 15th inning, the Mets filled the bases, and Robin Ventura swung hard. TV's Bob Costas called it this way: "A drive to right . . . back to Georgia . . . gone . . . a grand slam . . . a five-hour-47-minute trip to bedlam." It really wasn't a slam because teammates mobbed him after he touched first and kept him from reaching second. So the score read Mets 4, Braves 3.

Be as Great as Your Name

The Mets' stunning performance of 2000 came from Bobby Jones the pitcher in the fashion of Bobby Jones the legendary golfer.

The Mets' right-hander handled the San Francisco Giants with ease, 4-0, to give New York a 3-1 playoff series triumph. Jones was so effective at Shea, he held the hard-swinging Giants to one hit. It was nearly a perfect game, and that against the team that sported baseball's best record in 2000. The Giants loaded the bases in the fifth on Jeff Kent's double and two walks, but went down in order the other eight innings. It was the first one-hit shutout in the postseason since Boston's Jim Lonborg pulled it off in the 1967 World Series.

One Can Be One Big Number

Bob Murphy calls Bobby Jones' NL Division Series-clinching one-hitter on October 8, 2000: "Here's the pitch on the way to Bonds. . . . Fly ball to center. . . . Can he run it down? . . . On the run, Payton . . . makes the catch. . . . It's all over. . . . The Mets win it! Jay Payton makes the catch. . . . A one-hit shutout by Bobby Jones. . . . And they're all racing to the mound and mobbing Bobby Jones. . . . What a magnificent game. . . . The Mets have never had a better game pitched it their 39-year history than this game pitched by Bobby Jones."

When You Have Nails, Drive 'Em Home

They called him Nails. That's because Lenny Dykstra played hard and drove that point across. The blond Californian was a quick leadoff man, not your typical power-hitting center fielder. Yet when it counted most, Dykstra nailed 'em for the Mets. Game 3 of the 1986 NL Championship Series. The Mets and Astros were tied one game apiece. Houston led 5-4 in the ninth, with Wally Backman on second and one out. Up stepped Dykstra. Dave Smith tossed an 0-1 forkball. Bang. Dykstra nailed it—over the right-field wall for a 6-5 Mets triumph. Over 55,000 rocked Shea.

When It's Over, Call in Goodbye

Bob Murphy calls the winning homer in Game 3 of the NLCS on October 11, 1986: "Lenny Dykstra, the man they call Nails on the Mets ballclub, is waiting. . . . Now the pitch, and it's a high fly ball hit to right field. . . . It's fairly deep. . . . It's way back, by the wall. . . . A home run! A home run! The Mets win the ballgame. . . . Dykstra wins it. . . . Len Dykstra hit a home run. . . . This ballgame is over. . . . Lenny Dykstra is being mobbed by his teammates."

In 1962, Double 20 Meant Double Trouble

It wasn't easy pitching in front of Mets fielders in 1962. They flooded the field with 210 errors. Two pitchers had extra trouble. Roger Craig went 10-24 and Al Jackson 8-20. They were the first teammates to lose 20 since the 1936 Phillies tandem of Bucky Walters and Joe Bowman. Craig's reaction? "I had to be pretty good for them to keep sending me out there enough to lose that many games." Craig suffered again with the Mets in 1963, losing 22 games. But the next year he escaped to St. Louis and won a World Series game for the champion Cardinals.

Some Players Make
It Easy to Believe

Tug McGraw came up with one of the great rallying cries in sports history: "Ya Gotta Believe." He barked it during the Mets' rush of 1973, when they passed every team in the NL East on the way to their second division title.

McGraw, a left-handed relief pitcher, backed up his talk with 25 saves and a glove that he pounded against his leg while walking off the field. That was the memory McGraw left with Mets fans when they heard he died on January 5, 2004, of brain cancer at age 59.

Happiness Is Making a Long Season Pay Off

Bob Murphy's call of the 1973 Mets' 6-4, division-clinching victory at Wrigley Field in their last regular-season game: "Now the stretch by McGraw. . . . The 3-2 delivery. . . . The runner goes. . . . A little popup. . . . Milner's got it. . . . He'll run to first. . . . Double play! The Mets win the pennant! The Mets have just won the pennant in the Eastern Division! It's all over! They won the pennant with a magnificent stretch drive."

77

Ice 'Em With a Hot Arm

In 1973, the Mets surged down the stretch, yet won the NL East with just an 82-79 record. In the West, Cincinnati's Big Red Machine blew to the top at 99-63, baseball's best record that season. So the Reds' Game 1 victory over the Mets in the playoffs was quite expected. Game 2 wasn't. The Mets rebounded with a 5-0 triumph, thanks to masterful pitching by Jon Matlack. He kept the Reds to two hits, both by Andy Kosco. The rest of Cincy's sluggers—Pete Rose, Joe Morgan, Tony Perez, Johnny Bench—did nothing. Rusty Staub sure did. His fourth-inning homer was all the offense the Mets needed. Matlack, the lefty who was Rookie of the Year in 1972, fanned nine in this desperate Mets effort at Cincy's Riverfront Stadium. Instead of down 2-0, the Mets had the series tied. They went on to win in five games.

Take on the Big Guy and Beat Him

Before Tug McGraw relieved the winning Mets of 1969 and '73, he started for their earlier losing teams. McGraw's biggest accomplishment in those starting days? He was the first Met to beat Sandy Koufax.

McGraw handled the future Hall of Famer 5-2 on August 26, 1965, and that was no small feat. Koufax was 13-0 against the Mets going into that Shea showdown.

Tug wasn't always that fortunate. He went just 2-7 that rookie season of '65. Once he endured this mound exchange with manager Casey Stengel: "Skip, I know I can get this next guy. I've gotten him out twice already."

"Yeah—but you did it in this inning."

When You Have a Shot, Take It

Todd Pratt won't be mistaken as one of the Mets' greatest catchers. Yet, his chance came in Game 4 of the 1999 NL Division Series, and he grabbed it in dramatic fashion.

Pratt, a husky Nebraskan, was filling in for injured Piazza. The Mets and Arizona Diamondbacks were tied 3-3 in the 10th inning. One out, bases empty. Matt Mantei delivered a 1-0 fastball, and Pratt pasted it over the wall. When a leaping center fielder Steve Finley came down, looked in his glove and showed he hadn't caught it, 56,177 at Shea went bonkers.

Game over. Series over. The Mets won it three games to one. Pratt's homer was only the fourth to end a series after Pittsburgh's Bill Mazeroski in the 1960 World Series, the Yankees' Chris Chambliss in the 1976 AL championship and Toronto's Joe Carter in the 1993 World Series.

You Might Be Old, But Not Out

The greatest player to don Mets pinstripes was Willie Mays. The megastar of the New York and San Francisco Giants returned to the Big Apple in 1972 to wring out a couple of seasons with the Mets. Mays was 41 when he joined the Amazin's, but he looked like the Say Hey Kid in his first game back in New York. With 35,505 celebrating Mother's Day at Shea, Mays gave them the mother of all gifts, blasting a game-winning homer against—who else?—the Giants.

Great Ones Step Up Big

Willie Mays played 22 seasons of glorious baseball, with the last two years coming as a Met. This was his home stretch, yet he had enough to hit 14 of his 660 homers with the Amazin's. And on the biggest stage of all—the World Series—Mays had one last amazing moment in him.

It came in Game 2 in Oakland on October 14, 1973. With the Mets and A's tied 6-6 in the 12th inning, this 42-year-old wasn't about to fade in this late game. No way. Mays stepped up with two out and singled in Bud Harrelson with the go-ahead run in a 10-7 Mets triumph. Oakland went on to win the championship in seven games. So Mays ended his career the way he started it in 1951—on a New York National League team that made a mad rush for the pennant, then fell short in the World Series.

Name of the Game? Entertainment

One of the catchiest names in Mets history belonged to Choo Choo Coleman. Choo Choo was a Mets catcher in 1962 and '63, and returned for a few games in '66. The native of Orlando, Florida, hit just nine homers, but the man was quick. He was so impressive hustling down the line as a backstop, Phil Rizzuto once said, "He gets to first base before the batters do."

He wasn't so stellar behind plate. Mets pitcher Roger Craig once said, "Choo Choo would give you the sign and then look down to see what it was." At least he kept Mets fans laughing enough to attend games at the Polo Grounds to the tune of 922,530, a record at the time for a last-place team. On one broadcast, Ralph Kiner asked, "What's your wife's name and what is she like?" Choo Choo replied, "My wife's name is Mrs. Coleman and she likes me."

Name of the Game? Winning

Another zippy name on the Mets was Benny Agbayani. He roamed left field in New York from 1998 to 2001—one of the winningest runs in Mets history.

Agbayani came from Honolulu, and he came through in two exotic moments. On October 7, 2000, Agbayani homered in the 13th inning to win Game 3 of the NL Division Series against the San Francisco Giants. Shea shook with 56,270 partiers.

Seventeen days later, in Game 3 of the World Series at Shea, Agbayani doubled in the go-ahead run in the eighth inning as the Mets beat the Yankees 4-2. That would be the Mets' only victory of that Series.

First, Get Keith

The best trade the Mets ever made came on June 15, 1983. They sent shaky pitchers Neil Allen and Rick Ownbey to St. Louis for a fabulous first baseman: Keith Hernandez. The Mets were about to change from perennial chumps to champs.

Hernandez was a Cardinal force. He won the 1979 NL Most Valuable Player Award and led St. Louis to the 1982 World Series title. He combined a live bat with dead-solid defense, which explains his book title, *If at First*. Now he gave the Mets that force. Hernandez averaged nearly 90 RBIs the next four seasons and kept winning Gold Gloves at first. The Mets responded to his leadership by contending in 1984 and '85 and winning it all in 1986.

Make a Trade For the Ages

Jerry Koosman fired the last pitch of the 1969 World Series. When Baltimore's Davey Johnson lofted it to left and Cleon Jones caught it, the champion Mets mobbed Koosman on the mound. Jesse Orosco tossed the last pitch of the 1986 World Series. When Boston's Marty Barrett struck out, the champion Mets mugged Orosco on the mound.

Two lefties. Two World Series heroes. What else links Koosman and Orosco? The Mets sent Koosman to the Minnesota Twins for Orosco after the 1978 season. So the two Mets who were on the mound when they won their championships were traded for each other.

86

Second Is Fine, But Take First When It Counts

Jerry Koosman knew all about runner-up status. He won 19 games in 1968, yet finished behind Cincinnati's Johnny Bench in Rookie of the Year voting. He won 21 games in 1976, yet finished behind San Diego's Randy Jones on Cy Young ballots. And on the Mets' staff, Koosman was over-shadowed by the great Tom Seaver.

Yet in the postseason, Kooz was first and foremost clutch. In the 1969 World Series, he won both his starts, including the clinching Game 5. He went 1-0 in the 1973 World Series and 1-0 in that year's NL Championship Series. That adds up to a 100% result, second to none.

It Helps to Be Front and Center

Tommie Agee was the first black American to win the American League Rookie of the Year Award. He did so as a Chicago White Sox center fielder in 1966. Two years later he was on the Mets, and in 1969 his power and fielding prowess were cogs in the championship. He led the Miracle Mets with 26 homers and 76 RBIs.

His momentous regular-season performance came on September 8, 1969, at Shea. The Chicago Cubs were in town trying to hang on to their dwindling NL East lead. And their pitcher Bill Hands quickly fired a knockdown pitch at Agee. Tommie came back to homer and later score the go-ahead run on a wild play at the plate in a 3-2 Mets triumph. New York was suddenly just 1½ games behind and would soon charge ahead.

This Was the Age of Agee

The 1969 Mets displayed plenty of miracles. A few jumped out courtesy of Tommie Agee in Game 3 of the World Series. With 56,335 witnessing Shea Stadium's first World Series game, Agee led off with a homer.

Then he turned to defense. His sprinting, backhanded catch of Ellie Hendricks' smash stopped a Baltimore rally in the fourth inning. Agee came up big again in the seventh, diving to nab Paul Blair's liner with the bases loaded. Thanks to Agee, the Mets won 5-0 on the way to the title.

Stand Up for What's Right

Bud Harrelson was a skinny shortstop for the Mets—a lightweight at the plate and a heavyweight in the field. That heavy side weighed in during the 1973 NL Championship Series. It was Game 3, and the Mets were coasting to a 9-2 victory over the Cincinnati Reds. Pete Rose didn't like that predicament, so he slid hard into Harrelson amid a double play in the fifth inning.

When Rose and Harrelson got up, they confronted each other, and that led to both teams clearing the benches. When Rose later took his position in left field, Shea's fans fired debris at him. Harrelson and the Mets went on to knock out the Reds.

Can't Catch? Try Diving

Like so many Miracle Mets, shaky outfielder Ron Swoboda turned into a truly Amazin' player in 1969. His moment came in Game 4 of the World Series. The Mets led 1-0 with one out in the ninth. Frank Robinson stood on third and Boog Powell on first. Baltimore looked ready to swat Tom Seaver while 57,367 sweat at Shea.

Seaver delivered to Brooks Robinson, whose rope to right-center looked deadly. Except that a live Swoboda swooped in and caught it just off the grass. Frank Robinson tagged up and scored, but Swoboda's catch contained the rally, and the Mets won it 2-1 in the 10th.

"What made that a great play," TV analyst Jim Lampley said years later, "is Ron Swoboda made it."

Just Because Others Strike Out Doesn't Mean You Must

Ron Swoboda had one huge offensive game as the Mets sped toward their first title. It came on September 15, 1969, in St. Louis. The day seemed to belong to Cardinals lefty Steve Carlton, who struck out 19 Mets, a major league record at the time.

That didn't faze Swoboda. He tagged Carlton for a pair of two-run homers to lead the Mets to a 4-3 victory.

You Can Always Find Light

The Mets returned to their losing ways in the late 1970s. Only this time they didn't look Amazin'. Just amazingly bad. In the six full seasons from 1977 to '83, their average record was 66-96.

Shea fans didn't find it funny. As the Mets headed for a third straight last-place finish in 1979, attendance flopped to 9,740 a game, lower than at the Polo Grounds in '62.

Amid that gloom was a star: Lee Mazzilli. Here was a Brooklyn native with sharp looks and slick skills. He sped around center field and on the base paths, averaging 29 stolen bases from 1977 to '80. Mazzilli saved his highest time for that 1979 nadir. He hit .303 with 16 homers and 79 RBIs—and produced a 19-game hitting streak.

You Must Earn It

Craig Swan was another radiant player amid the Mets' dusk of the late 1970s and early '80s. The pitcher pulled the rare Mets coup of leading the National League. He did so with a 2.43 earned-run average in 1978, and that on a last-place team. Swan went 9-6 that year and followed at 14-13 in 1979 and 11-7 in '82, two more cellar-dweller Mets editions.

The Brightest Stars Keep Burning

Lee Mazzilli knew 1979 wasn't offering opportunities to perform in the clutch for the Mets. So he came through in the All-Star Game. It was held in Seattle, and Mazzilli woke up the National League. He homered to tie it in the eighth inning, then pushed across the go-ahead run by walking with the bases loaded in the ninth as the NL won 7-6.

That fiber helped feed the Mets a title years later. After stints with Texas, the Yankees and Pittsburgh, Mazzilli landed back on the Mets in time for their 1986 stretch run. In Game 6 of the World Series, with the Mets behind 3-2 in the eighth, who scored the tying run to make that historical 10th inning possible? Lee Mazzilli.

When You Step Up, Win in Grand Style

When it comes to mass production, Edgardo Alfonzo ripped the biggest hit in Mets postseason history. It came on October 5, 1999, in the NL Division Series in Phoenix.

The Mets were in a 4-4 Game 1 with the Arizona Diamondbacks, and up stepped Alfonzo in the ninth inning. The second baseman had already homered in the first inning. Now he faced reliever Bobby Chouinard with the bases loaded and two out. A 3-1 pitch. Tell it goodbye. Alfonzo's grand slam was the difference in an 8-4 victory for the Mets, who went on to beat Arizona in four games.

If You're Getting Rusty, Get Staub

After the power-hungry Mets landed right fielder Rusty Staub from the Montreal Expos in 1972, they found a man of many firsts. He powered them to first place in the National League in 1973. He gave the Mets their first 100-RBI man when he drove in 105 runs in 1975. He was the first major leaguer to amass 500 hits with four teams: Houston, Montreal, the Mets and Detroit. And when he returned to the Mets in 1981, he played first base.

Don't Let Pain Disarm You

Rusty Staub broke his hand in 1972, his first season with the Mets. He also hurt his shoulder while banging into the wall as he snared Dan Driessen's 11th-inning drive in Game 4 of the NL Championship Series.

Staub, which means "dust" in German, brushed off his injury fast. After hitting three homers to help beat Cincinnati in the playoffs, he led all regulars with 11 hits and a .423 average in the World Series. He even homered while going four for four with five RBIs in the Mets' 6-1 triumph in Game 4, although Oakland went on to win the championship.

98

You Want a Reliable Player Left In

John Franco was a local left-hander who had many right times for the Mets. Born in Brooklyn, he joined the Mets in 1990 and quickly saved the day. Coming out of the bullpen, he led the Mets in saves every season from '90 to '98. He peaked that last year with 38 saves.

Franco's biggest moment came in Game 3 of the 2000 World Series. He entered the eighth inning with a man on first, no outs, a 2-2 score and held the Yankees scoreless. He turned out to be the winning pitcher in the Mets' 4-2 triumph.

Throw Your Weight around When Your Big Time Comes

Al Weis stood 6 feet tall and weighed just 170 pounds. But did he ever bulk up when history called. The Mets' second baseman/shortstop hit just .215 with two homers in 1969's regular season.

Then came the pressure World Series, and did Weis ever turn white-hot. He led everyone with a .455 average and produced two crucial hits. In Game 2, Weis' two-out RBI single drove in Ed Charles with the go-ahead run in the ninth inning as the Mets won 2-1 and evened the Series. In Game 5, Weis' leadoff homer in the seventh tied it 3-3. The Mets vaulted from there to the title.

If You Can Win by a Foot, Do It

Mets legend Gil Hodges made one of the great managerial moves in history with his soft shoe in the 1969 World Series. It was Game 5. Shea's jammed 57,397 anticipated a title clincher.

Yet in the sixth inning, the Mets trailed 3-0. Cleon Jones led off and took an inside pitch. Hodges leapt at the opening. He took a ball to the umpire and pointed to shoe polish on the horse hide. Was Jones really hit by the pitch? Yes, said the ump, who awarded Jones first base.

Donn Clendenon followed with a two-run homer, and the Mets were on the way to a 5-3 victory. And Gil's gamers were champions, showing that you could go from setting the losing standard to the stratosphere before the decade was out—and by the same year men landed on the moon.

Leadership at the Top Sure Helps

"God is living in New York City and he's a Mets fan." That religious thought came from Tom Seaver, who had something to say about those 1969 Miracle Mets.

About the Author

Bucky Fox was born in Garden City, New York, and has been in love with the Mets since their heart-pounding season of 1969. He tuned in to that championship campaign on the radio while growing up in a U.S. military community in Germany. He caught the Mets' second title of 1986 again in Europe, this time while covering sports for the U.S. soldier newspaper *Stars & Stripes*. Fox is now an editor at *Investor's Business Daily* and runs an editing website, BuckyFox.com.